WILDERNESS

WILDERNESS

·THE LOST WRITINGS OF·

JIM MORRISON

VOLUME I

—

VINTAGE BOOKS
A DIVISION OF RANDOM HOUSE, INC.
NEW YORK

First Vintage Books Edition, december 1989

Copyright © 1988 by Wilderness Publications
Photographs copyright © 1988 by Frank J. Lisciandro

Library of Congress Cataloging-in-Publication Data
Morrison, Jim, 1943–1971.
    Wilderness: the lost writings of Jim Morrison.—1st Vintage
Books ed. 3| 16 5/2 8 //04
        p.   cm.
    ISBN 0-679-72622-5 (pbk. : v. 1)
    I. Title.
    [PS3563.08746W5   1989]
    811'.54—dc20   89-40163
                                                          CIP

Manufactured in the United States of America

9C

for Pamela Susan

I think I was once
I think we were

Your milk is my wine
My silk is your shine

Mosaic

a series of notes, prose-poems,
stories, bits of play & dialog
Aphorisms, epigrams, essays
poems? Sure

MOSAIC

a series of notes, prose-poems
stories, bits of play & dialog
Aphorisms, epigrams, essays

Poems? Sure

CONTENTS

PROLOGUE

SELF-INTERVIEW

I think the interview is the new art form. I think the self-interview is the essence of creativity. Asking yourself questions and trying to find answers. The writer is just answering a series of unuttered questions.

It's similar to answering questions on a witness stand. It's that strange area where you try and pin down something that happened in the past and try honestly to remember what you were trying to do. It's a crucial mental exercise. An interview will often give you a chance to confront your mind with questions, which to me is what art is all about. An interview also gives you the chance to try and eliminate all of those space fillers . . . you should try to be explicit, accurate, to the point . . . no bullshit. The interview form has antecedents in the confession box, debating and cross-examination. Once you say something, you can't really retract it. It's too late. It's a very existential moment.

I'm kind of hooked to the game of art and literature; my heroes are artists and writers.

I always wanted to write, but I always figured it'd be no good unless somehow the hand just took the pen and started moving without me really having anything to do with it. Like automatic writing. But it just never happened.

I wrote a few poems, of course. I think around the fifth or sixth grade I wrote a poem called "The Pony Express." That was the first I can remember. It was one of those ballad-type poems. I never could get it together though.

"Horse Latitudes" I wrote when I was in high school. I kept a lot of notebooks through high school and college, and then when I left school, for some dumb reason—maybe it was wise—I threw them all away. . . . I wrote in those books night after night. But maybe if I'd never thrown them away, I'd never have written anything original—because they were mainly accumulations of things that I'd read or heard, like quotes from books. I think if I'd never gotten rid of them I'd never been free.

Listen, real poetry doesn't say anything, it just ticks off the possibilities. Opens all doors. You can walk through any one that suits you.

. . . and that's why poetry appeals to me so much—because it's so eternal. As long as there are people, they can remember words and combinations of words. Nothing else can survive a holocaust but poetry and songs. No one can remember an entire novel. No one can describe a film, a piece of sculpture, a painting, but so long as there are human beings, songs and poetry can continue.

If my poetry aims to achieve anything, it's to deliver people from the limited ways in which they see and feel.

Jim Morrison
Los Angeles, 1969–71

POEMS
1966-1971

THE OPENING OF THE TRUNK

—Moment of inner freedom
when the mind is opened & the
infinite universe revealed
& the soul is left to wander
dazed & confus'd searching
here & there for teachers & friends.

Moment of Freedom
as the prisoner
blinks in the sun
like a mole
from his hole

a child's 1st trip
away from home

That moment of Freedom

LAmerica
Cold treatment of our empress
LAmerica
The Transient Universe
LAmerica
Instant communion and
                    communication
lamerica
emeralds in glass
lamerica
searchlights at twi-light
lamerica
stoned streets in the pale dawn
lamerica
robed in exile
lamerica   .
swift beat of a proud heart
lamerica
eyes like twenty
lamerica
swift dream
lamerica
frozen heart
lamerica
soldiers doom
lamerica
clouds & struggles
lamerica
Nighthawk

doomed from the start
lamerica
"That's how I met her,
lamerica
lonely & frozen
lamerica
& sullen, yes
lamerica
right from the start"

Then stop.
Go.
The wilderness between.
Go round the march.

he enters stage:

Blood boots. Killer storm.
Fool's gold. God in a heaven.
Where is she?
Have you seen her?
Has anyone seen this girl?
        snap shot (projected)
She's my sister.
Ladies & gentlemen:
    please attend carefully to these words & events
    It's your last chance, our last hope.
    In this womb or tomb, we're free of the
        swarming streets.
    The black fever which rages is safely
        out those doors
    My friends & I come from
    Far Arden w/dances, &
        new music
    Everywhere followers accrue
        to our procession.
    Tales of Kings, gods, warriors
        and lovers dangled like
        jewels for your careless pleasure

        I'm Me!

Can you dig it.
My meat is real.
My hands—how they move
balanced like lithe demons
My hair—so twined & writhing
The skin of my face—pinch the cheeks
My flaming sword tongue
spraying verbal fire-flys
I'm real.
I'm human
But I'm not an ordinary man
No No No

———————————————————

What are you doing here?
What do you want?
Is it music?
We can play music.
But you want more.
You want something & someone new.
Am I right?
Of course I am.
I know what you want.
You want ecstasy
Desire & dreams.
Things not exactly what they seem.
I lead you this way, he pulls that way.
I'm not singing to an imaginary girl.
I'm talking to you, my self.
Let's recreate the world.
The palace of conception is burning.

Look. See it burn.
Bask in the warm hot coals.

You're too young to be old
You don't need to be told
You want to see things as they are.
You know exactly what I do
Everything

I am a guide to the Labyrinth

Monarch of the protean towers
on this cool stone patio
above the iron mist
sunk in its own waste
breathing its own breath

———————————

POWER

I can make the earth stop in
its tracks. I made the
blue cars go away.

I can make myself invisible or small.
I can become gigantic & reach the
farthest things. I can change
the course of nature.
I can place myself anywhere in
space or time.
I can summon the dead.
I can perceive events on other worlds,
in my deepest inner mind,
& in the minds of others.

I can

I am

People need Connectors
   Writers, heroes, stars,
   leaders
To give life form.
A child's sand boat facing
   the sun.
Plastic soldiers in the miniature
   dirt war. Forts.
Garage Rocket Ships

Ceremonies, theatre, dances
To reassert Tribal needs & memories
a call to worship, uniting
above all, a reversion,
a longing for family & the
safety magic of childhood.

The grand highway
is
crowded
w/
lovers
&
searchers
&
leavers
so
eager
to
please
&
forget.

Wilderness

Now is blessed
The rest
remembered

A man rakes leaves into
a heap in his yard, a pile,
& leans on his rake &
burns them utterly.
The fragrance fills the forest
children pause & heed the
smell, which will become
nostalgia in several years

Sirens
Water
Rain & Thunder
Jet from the base
Hot searing insect cry
The frogs & crickets
Doors open & close
The smash of glass
The soft parade
An accident
Rustle of silk, nylon
Watering the dry grass
Fire
Bells
Rattle snake, whistles, castenets
Lawn mower
Good humor man
skates & wagons
Bikes

Sirens
Water
Rain & Thunder
Jet from the base
Hot searing insect cry
The frogs & crickets
Doors open & close
The smash of glass
The Soft Parade
An accident
Rustle of silk, nylon
Watering the dry grass
Fire
Bells
Rattlesnake, whistles, castanets
Lawn mower
Good Humor man
Skates & wagons
Bikes

Where'd you learn about
    Satan—out of a book
Love?—out of a box

night of sin (The Fall)
—1st sex, a feeling of having
done this same act in time before
O No, not again

Between childhood, boyhood,
                    adolescence
& manhood (maturity) there
should be sharp lines drawn w/
Tests, deaths, feats, rites
stories, songs, & judgements

Men who go out on ships
To escape sin & the mire of cities
watch the placenta of evening stars
from the deck, on their backs
& cross the equator
& perform rituals to exhume the dead
dangerous initiations
To mark passage to new levels

To feel on the verge of an exorcism
a rite of passage
To wait, or seek manhood
enlightenment in a gun

To kill childhood, innocence
in an instant

LAMERICA

Trade-routes
guide lines
The Vikings & explorers
Discoverers
The unconscious

a map of the states
The veins of hiways
Beauty of a map
Hidden connections
Fast trampled forest

Madness in a whisper
neon crackle
The hiss of tires
A city growls

rich vast & sullen
like a slow monster
come to fat
& die

THE ANATOMY OF ROCK

The 1st electric wildness came
over the people
on sweet Friday.
Sweat was in the air.
The channel beamed,
token of power.
Incense brewed darkly.
Who could tell then that here
it would end?

One school bus crashed w/a train.
This was the Crossroads.
Mercury strained.
I couldn't get out of my seat.
The road was littered
w/dead jitterbugs.
Help,
we'll be late for class.

The secret flurry of rumor
marched over the yard &
pinned us unwittingly
Mt. fever.
A girl stripped naked on the
base of the flagpole.

In the restrooms all was cool
& silent
w/the salt-green of latrines.
Blankets were needed.

Ropes fluttered.
Smiles flattered
& haunted.

Lockers were pried open
& secrets discovered.

Ah sweet music.

Wild sounds in the night
Angel siren voices.
The baying of great hounds.
Cars screaming thru gears
& shrieks
on the wild road
Where the tires skid & slide
into dangerous curves.

Favorite corners.
Cheerleaders raped in summer
buildings.
Holding hands
& bopping toward Sunday.

Those lean sweet desperate hours.

Time searched the hallways
for a mind.
Hands kept time.
The climate altered like a
visible dance.

Night-time women.
Wondrous sacraments of doubt
Sprang sullen in bursts
of fear & guilt
in the womb's pit hole
below
The belt of the beast

Worship w/words, w/
sounds, hands, all
joyful playful &
obscene—in the insane
infant.

———————

Old men worship w/long
noses, old soulful eyes.
Young girls worship,
exotic, indian, w/robes
who make us feel foolish
for acting w/our eyes.
Lost in the vanity of the senses
which got us where we are.
Children worship but seldom
act at it. Who needs
temples & couches & T.V.

We can do it on a sunny
floor w/friends & make
any sound or movement
that comes. Roll on our
backs screaming w/mirth
glad in the guilt of our
madness. Better to be
cool in our worship &
gain the respect of the
ancient & wise wearing
those robes. They know
the secret of mind-change
reality.

"Have you ever seen God?"
  —a mandala. A symmetrical angel.

Felt? yes. Fucking. The Sun.
Heard? Music. Voices
Touched? an animal. your hand.
Tasted? Rare meat, corn, water,
      & wine.

An angel runs
Thru the sudden light
Thru the room
A ghost precedes us
A shadow follows us
And each time we stop
We fall

No one thought up being;
he who thinks he has
Step forward

Shrill demented sparrows bark
The sun into being. They rule
dawn's Kingdom. The cars—
a rising chorus— Then
workmen's songs & hammers
The children of the schoolyard,
a hundred high voices,
complete the orchestration

"In that year there was
    an intense visitation
      of energy.
I left school & went down
    to the beach to live.
      I slept on a roof.
At night the moon became
    a woman's face.
I met the Spirit of Music."

An appearance of the devil
on a Venice canal.
Running, I saw a Satan
or Satyr, moving beside
me, a fleshy shadow
of my secret mind. Running,
Knowing.

The day I left the beach

A hairy satyr running
behind & a little to the
right.

On the holy solipsism
of the young?

Now I can't walk a ^{thru} city
street w/out eying each
single pedestrian. I feel
their vibes thru my
skin, the hair on my neck
— it rises.

The day I left the beach

A hairy Satyr running
behind & a little to the
right.

In the holy solipsism
    of the young

Now I can't walk thru a city
street w/out eying each
single pedestrian. I feel
their vibes thru my
skin, the hair on my neck
—it rises.

THE FEAR

Eternal consciousness
   in the Void
(makes trial & jail seem almost
            friendly)

a Kiss in the Storm

(Madman at the wheel
gun at the neck
space populous & arching
  coolly)

A barn
a cabin attic

Your own face
stationary
in the mirrored window

fear of restroom's
Tragic cold
neon

I'm freezing

animals
dead

white wings of
rabbits

grey velvet deer

The Canyon

The car a craft
in wretched
SPACE

Sudden movements

& your past
to warm you
in Spiritless
Night

The Lonely HWY
Cold hiker

Afraid of Wolves
& his own
Shadow

The Wolf,
who lives under the rock
has invited me
to drink of his cool
Water.
Not to splash or bathe
But leave the sun
& know the dead desert
                    night
& the cold men
    who play there.

a ha
Come on, now
luring the Traveller
Mighty Voyager
Curious, into its dark womb
The graves grinning
Indians of night
The eyes of night
Westward luring
into the brothel, into the blood bath
into the Dream
The dark Dream of conquest
& Voyage
into night, Westward into Night

L america

Clothed in sunlight
restless in wanting
dying of fever

changed shapes of an empire
Starling invaders
Vast promissary notes of joy

wanton, willful & passive
married to doubt
clothed in great warring monuments
of glory

How it has changed you
How slowly estranged you
Solely arranged you

Beg you for mercy

LAMERICA

Clothed in sunlight
restless in wanting
dying of fever

Changed shapes of an empire
Starling invaders
Vast promissory notes of joy

Wanton, willful & passive
Married to doubt
Clothed in great warring monuments
of glory

How it has changed you
How slowly estranged you
Solely arranged you

Beg you for mercy

The Crossroads
 a place where ghosts
 reside to whisper into
 the ear of travellers &
 interest them in their fate

Hitchhiker drinks:
"I call again on the dark
 hidden gods of the blood"

—Why do you call us?
 You know our price. It
 never changes. Death of
 you will give you life
 & free you from a vile
 fate. But it is getting late.

—If I could see you again
 & talk w/you, & walk a
 short while in your company,
 & drink the heady brew
 of your conversations,
 I thought

—to rescue a soul already
 ruined. To achieve respite.
 To plunder green gold
 on a pirate raid & bring
 to camp the glory of old.

—As the capesman faces
poisoned horns & drinks
red victory; the soldier,
too, w/his trophy, a
pierced helmet; & the
ledge-walker shuddering
his way into inward grace

—(laughter) Well then. Would
you mock yourself?

—No.

—Soon our voices must become
one, or one must leave.

Forest strong sandals
burnt geometry fingers
around a fire
reading history in blackened
books, charcoal sentence
in moot splendor

Flame-tree
Sire, we met in Eden
The troubled time
we had
rustling in the night leaves
a sniper aimed at our window
a kitten mewing in the blasted
strong air
I must go see

—You've found your Voice,
    friend, after all else
    I recognize fast the
    Strong sure tones of
    a poet
    was it a question
    search or of strangling?
    I wonder
    We never talked
    But welcome here
    to the camp fire
    Share our meal
    w/us
    & tell us of your life
    & the hanging

—Well 1st I screamed
  & I was a child again alive
  Then nothing til the age
  of 5

  & then summers & the racetrack
  I looked for a girl in
  New Mexican
  bars
  & found jail
  The prostitute looked out
  her cell & saw
  Fuck god scratched
  on a leprous wall

—You're rambling boy
  what of the rest
  the jazz hiway
  he winks.

—I got picked up
  & rode thru the night

—did you see any buildings

—did I . . .
  What was I doing
  of course we danced plenty
  She had nice sides
  the cop hit me
  Stop, I don't remember

—The logs are melting
  we must move on
  The fire's ending
  we'll hear more
  at the next altar

    [musical interlude]

Trees
Train-death
The American Night
We went thru 5 cords
  of wood this winter

—he told me beautiful stories
  & had the most beautiful visions
  He was a truly religious man
    at the end

—you know, I like you guys
   god–damn!

(I saw this cat run out
   of the ocean, one night,
and beat-off into a fire)

I'm going down to Mexico
To this border town I heard
about & I'm gonna buy
me a girl & bring her
back up here & marry her, it's
true. This guy told me.
A friend of his knew someone who

—You're too much

There was preserved
in her
The fresh miracle
of
surprise

open

The Night is young
               & full of rest
I can't describe the
               way she's dress'd
She'll pander to some strange
               requests
Anything that you suggest
Anything to please her guest

SIRENS

Midnight
criminal metabolism of guilt forest
Rattlesnakes whistles castanets

Remove me from this hall of mirrors
This filthy glass

Are you her
Do you look like that
How could you be when
no one ever could

———————————————————————

Poet of the call-girl storm

She left a note on the bedroom door.
"If I'm out, bring me to."

I dropped by to see you
        late last night
But you were out
        like a light
Your head was on the floor
& rats played pool w/your eyes

Death is a good disguise
for late at night

Wrapping all games in its calm garden

But what happens
when the guests return
& all unmask
& you are asked
to leave
for want of a smile

I'll still take you then
But I'm your friend

ODE
NEW YORK MAIDENS

everyone has Their own magic

There is no death

so nothing matters

High Style

Flash & forgive me

high button shoes

clean arrangement

messy breeding

love's triumph

everlasting hope & fulfillment

THE AMERICAN NIGHT

for leather accrues
    The miracle of the streets
The scents & smogs &
    pollens of existence

Shiny blackness
    so totally naked she was
    Totally un-hung-up

We looked around
    lights now on
To see our fellow travellers

I am troubled
Immeasurably
By your eyes

I am struck
By the feather
Of your soft
Reply

The sound of glass
Speaks quick
Disdain

And conceals
What your eyes fight
To explain

I am troubled
Immeasurably
By your eyes

I am struck
By the feather
of your soft
Reply

The sound of glass
Speaks quick
Disdain

And conceals
What your eyes fight
To explain

She looked so sad in sleep
Like a friendly hand
    just out of reach
A candle stranded on
    a beach
While the sun sinks low
    an H-bomb in reverse

Everything human
   is leaving
      her face

Soon she will disappear
   into the calm
      vegetable
         morass

Stay!

My Wild Love!

I get my best ideas when the
telephone rings & rings. It's no fun
To feel like a fool—when your
baby's gone. A new ax to my head:
Possession. I create my own sword
of Damascus. I've done nothing w/time.
A little tot prancing the boards playing
w/Revolution. When out there the
World awaits & abounds w/heavy gangs
of murderers & real madmen. Hanging
from windows as if to say: I'm bold—
do you love me? Just for tonight.
A One Night Stand. A dog howls & whines
at the glass sliding door (why can't I
be in there?) A cat yowls. A car engine
revs & races against the grain—dry
rasping carbon protest. I put the book
down—& begin my own book.
Love for the fat girl.
When will SHE get here?

In the gloom
In the shady living room
where we lived & died
& laughed & cried
& the pride of our relationship
took hold that summer
What a trip
To hold your hand
& tell the cops
you're not 16
no runaway
The wino left a little in
    the old blue desert
          bottle
Cattle skulls
    the cliché of rats
who skim the trees
in search of fat
Hip children invade the grounds
    & sleep in the wet grass
     'til the dogs rush out
I'm going South!

MIAMI

What can I read her
What can I read her
    on a Sunday Morning

What can I do that will
    somehow reach her
    on a Sunday Morning

I'll read her the news of
        The Indian Wars

Full of criss-cavalry, blood
        & gore

Stories to tame & charm
        & more

On a Sunday Morning

Some wild fires
Searchout
a dry quiet kiss on leaving

Like our ancestors
The Indians
We share a fear of sex
excessive lamentation for the dead
& an abiding interest in dreams & visions

Explosion

The mushroom
the unfolding

instant of creation (fertilisation
    not an instant seperate from breakfast
    it all flows down + out, flowing

but that instant :
    not fire + fusion (fission) but a moment
    of jellied ice, crystal, vegetative mating
    merging in cool slime splendour.
    a crushing of steel + glass + ice

    (instant in a bar; glasses clash, clink, collid

far-out splendour

heat + fire are outwards signs of a
small dry mating

===========

EXPLOSION

The mushroom
The unfolding

instant of creation (fertilisation)
    not an instant separate from breakfast
    It all flows down & out, flowing

but that instant:
    not fire & fusion (fission) but a moment
    of jellied ice, crystal, vegetative mating
    merging in cool slime splendour
    a crushing of steel & glass & ice

    (instant in a bar; glasses clash, clink, collide)

    far-out splendour

    heat & fire are outwards signs of a
    Small dry mating

event in a room
event in space
a circle
Magic rite
To call up the godhead
spirits, demons
The shaman calls:
"When radio dark night . . ."
We are eating each other.

————————————————

The Voice of the Serpent
    dry hiss of age & steam
     & leaves of gold
        old books in ruined
         Temples
        The pages break like ash

I will not disturb
I will not go

Come, he says softly

an old man appears &
  moves in tired dance
  amid the scattered dead
gently they stir

I received an Aztec wall
of vision
& dissolved my room in
sweet derision
Closed my eyes, prepared to go
A gentle wind inform'd me so
And bathed my skin in ether glow

I received an Aztec wall
                    of vision
& dissolved my room in
                    sweet derision
Closed my eyes, prepared to go
A gentle wind inform'd me so
And bathed my skin in ether glow

Drugs are a bet w/your mind

The cigarette burn'd
         my fingertips
& dropp'd like a log
         to the rug below
My eyes took a trip
         to dig the chick
Crouch'd like a cat
         at the next window
My ears assembled music
         out of swarming streets
but my mind rebelled
            at the idiot's laughter
The rising frightful idiot laughter
Cheering an army of
         vacuum cleaners

Mouth fills w/taste of copper.
Chinese paper. Foreign money. Old posters.
Gyro on a string, a table.
A coin spins. The faces.

There is an audience to our drama.
Magic shade mask.
Like the hero of a dream, he works for us,
in our behalf.

How close is this to a final cut?

I fall. Sweet blackness.
Strange world that waits & watches.
Ancient dread of non-existence.

If it's no problem, why mention it.
Everything spoken means that,
its opposite, & everything else.
I'm alive. I'm dying.

1st wild thrush of fear

—A phone rings
 There is a knock on the door.
 It's time to go.
 No.

Jail

The walls screamed poetry disease & sex
an inner whine like a mad machine

The Computer

faces of the men

The wall collage
  reading matter

  The Traders (dealers)

dropped in a
cave of roaches
or rodents

JAIL

The walls screamed poetry disease & sex
an inner whine like a mad machine
The Computer
faces of the men

The wall collage
    reading matter

The Traders (dealers)

                    dropped in a
                    cave of roaches
                    or rodents

I am a guide to the labyrinth
Come & see me
in the green hotel
Rm. 32
I will be there after 9:30 P.M.

I will show you the girl of the ghetto
I will show you the burning well
I will show you strange people
    haunted, beast-like, on the
    verge of evolution

—Fear The Lords who are
    secret among us

Leaving the phone-booth, I was
Struck by a whiff of
      the weird.
Insane old country woman
  come to nag the haunts
     of town
Hairy legs w/open sores.

From what swamp or under-rock
  did you crawl to remind
   us what we choose
    to leave

———————————————————————

L America

Androgynous, liquid, happy
Heavy
Facile & vapid
Weighted w/ words
Mortgaged soul
wandering preachers, & Delta tramps

Box-cars of heaven
New Orleans Nile sunset

LAmerica

Androgynous, liquid, happy
Heavy
Facile & vapid
Weighted w/words
Mortgaged soul
Wandering preachers, & Delta Tramps

Box-cars of heaven
New Orleans Nile Sunset

The form is a plane above
the earth. A soldier bails
out, leaving his entrails
fluttering, billowing. Scoop'd
down, windy midwife, wrench'd
by the world from her rich
belly, my metal mother,
ripped cord, down & frozen.
Following pilot the eye of
the plane; "Great Eye of Night"
God on a windscreen, wind—
scream, wormwind
Trailing.

   (& hide among women
     like a toothless bird)

Burned by air
Burned bad by light
in the

     [gun shot]

O Wow
he's shot
& the scarlet news
  (hoarse mute confusion
   of the witness crowd)

Airport.
Messenger in the form of a soldier.
Green wool. He stood there,
off the plane.
A new truth, too horrible to bear.
There was no record of it
anywhere in the ancient signs
or symbols.
People looked at each other,
in the mirror, their children's
eyes.
Why had it come.
There was no escape from
it anywhere.
A truth too horrible to name.
Only a loose puking moan
could frame its dark interiors.
Only a few could look upon
its face w/calm.
Most of the people fell instantly
under its dull friendly terror.
They looked to the calm ones
but saw only a green
military coat.
Repent!
None of the old Things worked.

disciple
Scar
death
Magic
Prison
Garden
Shelter
Princess
  of Sorrow
Wilderness Angel
dancing wings
  of envy
Call Me
Tomorrow
Bones
Landing
Gold
Arrival

Street. Steel thrust sucking space.
Silent willful turbines, motors
raving

City of clouds, pirates of air.

Land of rainbows & scarlet rare
                              islands.

We are here, parables.

Silent climbers.

The breast engine mattered.
Monster in drag, a tin damsel
Shuddered & flew

Cut spent space
Crazed ace
Collect

The cake-walk.

HORSE LATITUDES

The barn is burning
The race-track is over
Farmers run out w/
buckets of water
The horse flesh is burning
They're kicking the stalls
(panic in a horse's eye
That can spread & fill
an entire sky.)

The clouds flow by
& tell a story

about the lightning bolt & the mast
on the steeple

Some people have a hard time
describing sailors to the
undernourished.

The decks are starving
Time to throw the cargo over

Now down & the high-sailing
fluttering of smiles on the air
w/its cool night time disturbance

Tropic corridor
Tropic Treasure

What got us this far to this
mild equator

Now we need something
          & someone new
when all else fails
we can whip the horse's eyes
         & make them cry
            & sleep

France is 1st, Nogales round-up
Goss over the border —
land of eternal adolescence
quality of despair unmatched
anywhere on the perimeter
Message from the outskirts
calling us home
This is the private space of a
new order. We need saviours
To help us survive the journey.
Now who will come
Now hear this
We have started the crossing
Who knows? it may end badly

The actors are assembled;
immediately they become
enchanted ~~& the sun~~
~~~~
I, for one, am in ecstasy
enthralled.
Can I convince you to smile?

No wise men now.
Each on his own
grab your daughters & run

France is 1st, Nogales round-up
Cross over the border—
land of eternal adolescence
quality of despair unmatched
anywhere on the perimeter
Message from the outskirts
calling us home
This is the private space of a
new order. We need saviors
To help us survive the journey.
Now who will come
Now hear this
We have started the crossing
Who knows? it may end badly

The actors are assembled;
immediately they become
enchanted
I, for one, am in ecstasy
enthralled.
Can I convince you to smile?

No wise men now.
Each on his own
grab your daughter & run

"Oh God, she cried
I never knew what
it meant to be real
I thought all this was a joke,
I never let the horror, or
the sweetness & the dignity
penetrate my brain"

"Let me up to see
the window. Dark Riders
pass in the sunset
coming home from
raiding parties.
The taverns will be
full of laughter, wine,
& later dancing, later
dangerous knife throws.

Antonio will be there
& that whore, Blue Lady
playing cards w/silver
decks & smiling at the night,
& full glasses held aloft
& spilled to the moon.
I'm sad, so full of sadness"

She's selling news in the market
Time in the hall
The girls of the factory
Rolling cigars
They haven't invented musak yet
So I read to them
From The BOOK OF DAYS
a horror story from the Gothic age
a gruesome romance
From the LA
Plague.

I have a vision of America
Seen from the air
28,000 ft. & going fast

A one-armed man in a Texas
                    parking labyrinth
A burnt tree like a giant primeval bird
              in an empty lot in Fresno
Miles & miles of hotel corridors
& elevators, filled w/citizens

Motel Money Murder Madness
Change the mood from glad to sadness

        play the ghost song baby

a young woman, bound silently, on
a hospital table, obviously pregnant,
is gutted & rifled of her empire

objects of oblivion

Drugs sex drunkenness battle
return to the water-world
Sea-belly
Mother of man
Monstrous sleep-waking gentle swarming
    atomic world
Anomie in social life

how can we hate or love or judge
    in the sea-swarm world of atoms
    All one, one All
How can we play or not play
How can we put one foot before us
    or revolutionize or write

Does the house burn? So be it.
The World, a film which men devise.
Smoke drifts thru these chambers
Murders occur in a bedroom.
Mummers chant, birds hush & coo.
Will this do?
Take Two.

each day is a drive thru history

Bright Flags

The great hiway of dawn
Stretching to slumber
pouring out from his greedy
palms a shore, to wander

Hesitation & doubt
swiftly ensconced

O Viking, your women
cannot save you
out on the great ship

Time has claimed you
Coming for you

BRIGHT FLAGS

The great hiway of dawn
Stretching to slumber
pouring out from her greedy
palms a shore, to wander

Hesitation & doubt
Swiftly ensconced

O Viking, your women
cannot save you
out on the great ship

Time has claimed you
Coming for you

And I came to you
            for peace
And I came to you
            for gold
And I came to you
            for lies
And you gave me fever
            & wisdom
            & cries
            of sorrow
& we'll be here
            the next day
            the next day
            &
            Tomorrow

There's a belief by the
Children of Man which states
all will be well

Search on man, calm savior
Veteran of wars incalculable
greed. Search on man, calm savior
God-speed & forgive you
morning-star, fragrant
meadow person girl

UNDERWATERFALL

down
  down
    down
      down
        down
          down
            deep
              below

children of the caves will let their
             secret fires glow

An explosion of birds
Dawn
Sun strokes the walls
An old man leaves the Casino
A young man reading pauses
on the path to the garden

Bitter winter
Fiction dogs are starving
The radio is moaning softly
           calling to the dogs
There are still a few
           animals left in the yard

Sit up all night,
           talking smoking
Count the dead & wait
           'til morning
Will warm names & faces
           come again
Does the silver forest end?

December Isles
Hot morning chambers
    of the New Day
Idiot first to awaken (be born)
w/shadows of new play
learned men
in Sunday best
we've had our chance to rest
to mourn the passing of day
to lament the death of our
glorious member
    (she whispers secret messages
       of love in the garden
        to her friends, the bees)
The garden would be here
forevermore

Mexican parachute
Blue green pink
Invented of Silk
& stretched on grass
Draped in the trees
of a Mexican Park
T-shirt boys in their
Slumbering art

—I fear that he's been
   maim'd beyond all
   recognition

He hears them come &
   murmur over his corpse.

Street Pizza.

funny,
    I keep expecting a
knock on the door
well, that's what you
get for living around
          people

a Knock? would shatter
     my dreams' illusions
        deportment & composure
The struggle of a poor poet
     to stay out of the grips
    of novels & gambling
        & journalism

A quality of ignorance,
self-deception may be
necessary to the poet's
survival.

Actors must make us think
They're real
Our friends must not
make us think we're acting

They
~~act~~ are, though, in slow
Time

My wild words
slip into fusion
& risk losing
The solid ground

So stranger, get
wilder still!

Probe The Highlands

Actors must make us think
they're real
Our friends must not
make us think we're acting

They are, though, in slow
Time

My wild words
slip into fusion
& risk losing
the solid ground

So stranger, get
wilder still

Probe the Highlands

Bourbon is a wicked brew, recalling
courage milk, refined poison
of cockroach & tree-bark, leaves
& fly-wings scraped from the
land, a thick film; menstrual
fluids no doubt add their splendour.
It is the eagle's drink.

Why do I drink?
So that I can write poetry.

Sometimes when it's all spun out
and all that is ugly recedes
into a deep sleep
There is an awakening
and all that remains is true.
As the body is ravaged
the spirit grows stronger.

Forgive me Father for I know
what I do.
I want to hear the last Poem
of the last Poet.

THE CONNECTORS

—What is connection?

—When 2 motions, thought
to be infinite & mutually
exclusive, meet in a
moment.

—Of Time?

—Yes.

—Time does not exist.
There is no time.

—Time is a straight plantation.

———————————————————

THE CONNECTORS

The diamonds shone like broken glass
Upon the midnight street
And all atop the walls were wet
Their white eyes glint & sleek

Then from afar a gnome appeared
An angel flashed on furry feet
The boulevard became a river
While waiting crowds began to quiver

I was in a motel watching
Whiskey in my hand
Her breath was soft, the wind was warm
Someone in a room was born

Accomplishments:

To make works in the face
                of the void
To gain form, identity
To rise from the herd-crowd

Public favor
public fervor

even the bitter Poet-Madman is
                a clown
Treading the boards

Cold electric music
    Damage me
Rend my mind
    w/your dark slumber

Cold temple of steel
    Cold minds alive
        on the strangled shore

Veterans of foreign wars
    We are the soldiers of
        Rock & Roll Wars

Whether to be a
    great cagey perfumed
    beast
dying under the
    sweet patronage
    of kings
& exist like luxuriant
flowers beneath the
emblems of their
    strange empire
or by mere insouciant
        faith
    slap them, call their cards
spit on fate & cast help-
to flames into the luxuri
        us

Whether to be a
       great cagey perfumed
       beast
    dying under the
       sweet patronage
       of Kings
& exist like luxuriant
    flowers beneath the
    emblems of their
       Strange empire
or by mere insouciant
                 faith
    slap them, call their cards
spit on fate & cast hell
to flames in usury

by dying, nobly
    we could exist like
innocent trolls
    propagate our revels
& give the finger to the
    gods in our private
       bedrooms

let's rather, maybe,
       perhaps,
    get fucking out in
       the open, & by
    swelling, jubilantly
Magnificently, end them.

Ode to LA
while thinking of
Brian Jones, Deceased

I'm a resident of a city
They've just picked me to play
the Prince of Denmark

Poor Ophelia

All those ghosts he never saw
Floating to doom
On an iron candle

Come back, brave warrior
Do the dive
On another channel

Hot buttered pool
Where's Marrakesh
Under the falls
the wild storm
where savages fell out
in late afternoon
monsters of rhythm

You've left your
Nothing
to compete w/
Silence

I hope you went out
Smiling
Like a child
Into the cool remnant
of a dream

The angel man
w/Serpents competing
for his palms
& fingers
Finally claimed
This benevolent
Soul

Ophelia

Leaves, sodden
in silk

Chlorine
dream
mad stifled
Witness

The diving board, the plunge
The pool

You were a fighter
a damask musky muse

You were the bleached
Sun
for TV afternoon

horned-toads
maverick of a yellow spot

Look now to where it's got
You

in meat heaven
w/the cannibals
& jews

The gardener
Found
The body, rampant, Floating

Lucky Stiff
What is this green pale stuff
You're made of

Poke holes in the goddess
Skin

Will he Stink
Carried heavenward
Thru the halls
of music

No chance.

Requiem for a heavy
That smile
That porky satyr's
leer
has leaped upward

into the loam

FAR ARDEN

In that year
We had an intense visitation
                    of energy

SIGNALS

When radio dark night existed
& assumed control, & we rocked in its web
consumed by static, & stroked w/fear
we were drawn down long from
a deep sleep, & awaken'd
at dayfall by worried guardeners
& made to be led thru dew wet
jungle to the swift summit, o'er looking
The sea. . . .

A vast radiant beach & a cool
jewelled moon. Couples naked
race down by its quiet side &
we laugh like soft mad children,
smug in the wooly cotton brains
of infancy.

The music & voices are all around us.

Choose, They croon
The ancient ones
The time has come again
Choose now, They croon
Beneath the moon
Beside an ancient lake

Enter again the sweet forest
Enter the hot dream, come w/us
Everything is broken up
& dances

                    (Mt. Music
                        Violin)

Moonshine night
Mt. Village
Insane in the woods
     in the deep trees

Under the moon
Beneath the stars
They reel & dance
The young folk

Led to the Lake
by a King & Queen

O, I want to be there
I want us to be there
Beside the lake
Beneath the moon
Cool & swollen
dripping its hot
liquor

SSSSSSSSSSSSSSSSSSS

Frozen moment by a lake
A Knife has been stolen
The death of the snake

I know the impossible sea
    when the dogs bark

I am a death bird
    Naughty night bird

———————————————

Bird of prey, Bird of prey
flying high, flying high
In the summer sky

Bird of prey, Bird of prey
flying high, flying high
Gently pass on by

Bird of prey, Bird of prey
flying high, flying high
Am I going to die

Bird of prey, Bird of prey
flying high, flying high
Take me on your flight

Indians scattered on dawn's
Hiway bleeding.
Ghosts crowd the young child's
    fragile egg-shell mind

Underwaterfall, Underwaterfall
The girls return from summer balls
Let's steal the eye that sees us all

TAPE NOON

Tell them you came & saw & looked
into my eyes, & saw the shadow
of the guard receding
Thoughts in time & out of season
The hitchhiker stood by the side of the road
& levelled his thumb in the
calm calculus of reason

      (a car passes)

Why does my mind circle around you
Why do planets wonder what it
Would be like to be you

All your soft wild promises were words
Birds, endlessly in flight

Your dog is still lost in the frozen woods
or he would run to you
How can he run to you
Lunging w/blooded sickness on the snow
He's still sniffing gates & searching
Strangers for your smell
which he remembers very well

Is there a moon in your window
Is madness laughing
Can you still run down beach
rocks bed below w/out him?

    Winter Photography
    our love's in jeopardy
    Winter Photography
    our love's in jeopardy
Sit up all night, talking smoking
    Count the dead & wait for morning
(Will warm names & faces come again
    Does the silver forest end?)

ORANGE COUNTY SUITE

Well I used to know someone fair
She had orange ribbons in her hair
She was such a trip
She was hardly there
But I loved her
Just the same.

There was rain in our window,
The FM set was ragged
But she could talk, yeah,
We learned to speak

And one year
has gone by

Such a long long road to seek it
All we did was break and freak it
We had all
That lovers ever had
We just blew it
And I'm not sad

Well I'm mad

And I'm bad

And two years
have gone by

Now her world was bright orange
And the fire glowed
And her friend had a baby
And she lived with us
Yeah, we broke through the window
Yeah, we knocked on the door
Her phone would not answer,
Yeah, but she's still home

Now her father has passed over
& her sister is a star
& her mother smokes diamonds
& she sleeps out in the car

Yeah, but she remembers Chicago
The musicians & guitars
& grass by the lake
& people who laugh'd
& made her poor heart ache

Now we live down in the valley
We work out on the farm
We climb up to the mountains
& everything's fine

& I'm still here
& you're still there
& we're still around

Well I'll tell you a story of whiskey
   & mystics & men
And about the believers, & how the
   whole thing began

First there were women & children obeying
                       the moon
Then daylight brought wisdom & fever
              & sickness too soon

You can try to remind me
   instead of the other
            you can

You can help to insure
   That we all insecure our command

If you don't give a listen
   I won't try to tell your
           new hand

This is it can't you see
   That we all have our end in
          the band

And if all of the teachers & preachers
        of wealth were
                arraigned

We could see quite a future
for me in the literal sands

And if all of the people
        could claim to inspect
                such regret

Well we'd have no forgiveness
        forgetfulness faithful
                remorse

So I tell you
        I tell you
        I tell you
We must send away

We must try to find a new
        answer instead of
                a way

All hail the American Night

And so I say to you
The silk handkerchief was
embroidered in China or Japan
behind the steel curtain   And
no one can cross the borderline
w/out proper credentials.
This is to say that we are all
sensate & occasionally sad
& if every partner in crime
were to incorporate promises
in his program the dance
might end & all our friends
would follow.

Who are our friends?

Are they sullen & slow?   Do
they have great desire?   Or
are they one of the multitude who
walk doubting their impossible
regret.   Certainly things happen
& reoccur in continuous promise;
All of us have found a safe
niche where we can store up
riches & talk to our fellows
on the same premise of disaster.

But this will not do.   No, this
will never do.   There are
continents & shores which
beseech our understanding.
Seldom have we been so slow.
Seldom have we been so far.

My only wish is to see
Far Arden again.

The truth is on his chest
The cellular excitement has
Totally inspired our magic
Veteran.   And now for an
old trip.   I'm tired of thinking.
I want the old forms to
reassert their sexual cool.
My mind is just—you know.
And this morning before I sign
off I would like to tell you
about Texas Radio & the Big Beat.
It moves into the perimeter of
your sacred sincere & dedicated
Smile like a calm survivor
of the psychic war.   He was
no general for he was not old.
He was no private for he
could not be sold.

He was only a man & his
dedication extended to the last
degree.   Poor pretentious soldier,
come home.   The dark Los Angeles
evening is steaming the Church
that we attended & I miss
my boy.   Stupid in green—
What the color green?   When
I watch the T.V. & I see
helicopters swirling their
brutal & bountiful sensation
over the fields & the comic walls
I can only smile & fix a meal
& think about the child who
will one day own you.

In conclusion, darling, let
me repeat: your home is still
here, inviolate & certain
and I open the wide smile of
my remembrance.   This to you
on the anniversary of our first
night.   I know you love me
to talk this way.   I hope
no one sees this message
written in the calm lonely
far out languid summer afternoon
W/my total love

JAMAICA

The hour of the wolf
has now ended. Cocks
crow. The world is built
up again, struggling in
darkness.

The child gives in to night–
Mare, while the grown
Man fears his fear.

I must leave this island,
Struggling to be born
from blackness.

Fear the good deep dark
American Night.
Blessed is Night.

The flood has subsided
The movie panic & the
chauffeured drive
Thru the suburbs

Wild folks in weird dress
by the side of the hiway

Some of the men wear
Tunics or short skirts.
The women posture on
Their porches in mock-
classical pose.

The driver aims the car
& it guides itself. Tunnels
click by overhead.

Love the deep green gloom
of American Night.

Love frightened corners,
Thrill to the wood-vine.

So much of it good
& so much quantity.

———————

The Major's boots are where
he left them.

Pseudo-plantation.

Period prints—white
& black boxing match.

A Negro Dance

———————

The principal of the school holds his nose.
"A dead cow is in there. I wonder
why they haven't sent someone to
remove it?"

A vulture streams by,
& another. The white tip
of his claw-like red beak
looks white, like meat.
Swift sad languorous
shadows.

The cat drinks little cat
laps from a sick
Turquoise swimming pool.

(Insane couplings out in the night.)

America, I am hook'd to your
Cold white neon bosom, & suck
snake-like thru the dawn, I
am drawn back home
your son in exile
in the land of Awakening
What dreams possessed you
To merge in the morning?

"I been in a daze"

A spot, a reef, behind
the nursery door, off
the main bedroom—
"Those are the major's."

The bed looms like a white
funereal butterfly barge
at one end of the room,
hung w/nets & sails.

"We're outlaws."

"What church is that?"
"Church of God."
white bandana, white tambourine

—Walking on the Water—

"In traditional style, we'll
give them a good political
back-siding"—(laughter)

"Victimization"

a frog in the road
children in church
drums
Sun–Sun
lying like death
on the back seat
Revival.

A whore-house.
Lord John & Lady Anne's.
Red-blooded Blue-blooded.
Queen's bosom.
Is it The Princess?

Golden-blood, like me, he said,
folding the bill again neatly,
the Queen's ear—a naked
cock stuck in her ass.

Ha Ha Ha Ha.

You're no more innocent
than a turkey vulture

A cannon.

The Negro slaves & the English
killed the Indians, & mixed
w/the Spanish, who were soon
forced out.

Yes, big battles

Boom Boom.

DRY WATER

The velvet fur of religion
The polish of knife handle & coin
The universe of organic gears
or microscope mechanical
embryo metal doll
The night is a steel machine
grinding its slow stained wheels
The brain is filled w/clocks, & drills
& water down drains
Knife-handle, thick blood
like the coin & cloth
they rub & the skin they love
to touch

the graveyard, the tombstone,
the gloomstone & runestone
The sand & the moon, mating
deep in the Western night
waiting for the escape
of one of our gang
The hangman's noose is a
silver sluice bait
come-on man
your meat is hanging
on the wing of the raven
man's bird, poet's soul

Shhhhhhhhhhhhhhh
the thin rustle of weeds
the voice comes from faraway
inside, awaiting its birth
in a cool room, on tendril bone
The insane free chummy cackle
of infants in a ballroom, of a
family of friends around
a table, laden w/feast-food
soft guilty female laughter
the bar-room, the men's room
people assemble to establish
armies & find their foe
& fight

Clustered in watchful terror
by vine-growth, the hollow bush
    dry cancerous wells
We awoke before dawn, slipped
    into the canyon

Noon schoolyard screamed
    w/play, the lunch hour ending
ropes & balls slapped hard at
    cement sand, the female land
was bright, all swelling to degree
    most comfortless & guarding

A record noise shot out
    & stunned the earth. The music
had been bolted w/new sound.
    Run, run the end of repose
an anthem has churned
    the bad guys are winning.

Silver shaken in the gloom
I left her

Trees waste & sway forever

Marble porch & sylvan frieze
Down on her knees

She begs the spider-king to wed her
Slides into bed

He turns her over

There is a leather pouch
that's full of silver

It spills like water

She left
And took the coins I gave her

As to the drowning man
hoarse whisper
invokes, on the edge,
an arroyo
Sangre de Christo

Violence in a time of plenty

There is one deaf witness
on the bank, the shore
leaning in finery against
a ruined wall
as Jesus did. Red livid lips,
pale flesh withdrawn from
ragged dress, pit of the past
& secrets unveiled in the
scarred chalk wall

When, often, one is not deluged
by rain, 3 drops suffice
The war is over there
I am neither doctor nor saint
Christ or soldier
Now, friends, don't look at me
sadly ranting like some
incomprehensible child
I know by my breath of what
I speak, & what I've seen
needs telling.

Please, freeze!
Danger near.
A message has started its path
to the heart of the brain
A thin signal is on its way
An arrow of hope, predicting rain
A death-rod bearing pain

I

I will not come again
I will not come again
into the swirl
The bitter wine-soaked
stallion eats the seed,
all labor is a lie;
no vice is kindled in
these loins to melt
or vie w/any strong
particulating smile.
Leave sundry stones alive.

II

Now that you have gone
all alone
the desert to explore
& left me here alone

the calmness of the town
where a girl in black
gets in a car
& searches numbly
for her keys;

Now that you have gone
or strayed away—

I sit, & listen to the hiss
of traffic & invoke
into this burned & gutted
room some ghost, some
vague resemblance of a time

Off–on, on and off,
like one long sick
electric dream.
This state is confused
state. Out there everyone
is greedy for her love.

They will drain her life
like warm connectors,
plug into her soul
From every side & melt
her form for me.

But I deserve this,
Greatest cannibal of all.
Some tired future.
Let me sleep.
Get on w/the disease.

THE VILLAGE TAPES

POEMS RECORDED
DECEMBER 7, 1970

Come
for all the world lies
hushed & fallen
green ships dangle
on the surface of
Ocean, & sky–birds
glide smugly among
the planes
Gaunt crippled houses
Strangle the cliffs
In the East, in the cities
a hum of life
begins, now come

Of the Great Insane
American Night
We sing
sending our gift
to its vast promise

Pilots are a problem
The rain & hungry sea
greedy for steel

Say a soft American Prayer
A quiet animal sigh
for the strong plane
landing

We rode on opium tires
from the colossal
airport chess game
at dawn, new from glass
in the broken night

landed then in quiet
fog, beside the times
out of this strange river

Then gladly thru
a wasted morning
happy to be alive to
signs of life
a dog,
a school girl
are we in Harlem?

Blessings

accept this ancient
wisdom
which has travelled
far to greet us
From the East
w/the sun

Call out to him
From the mountain
high, from high
towers

as the mind
rebels
& wends its way
to freedom

grant us one more day
& hour
the hero of this dream
who heals & guides us

Forgive me, Blacks
you who unite
as I fear & gently
fall on darkness

SCIENCE OF NIGHT

Earth Air Fire Water
Mother Father Sons & Daughters
Airplane in the starry night
First fright
Forest follow free
I love thee
watch how I love thee

The Politics of ecstasy are real
Can't you feel them working
thru you
Turning night into day
Mixing sun w/the sea.

Lakes domain
wilderness pain
cruel swimming ambience
sweet swimming fishhook smile
I love you all the while
even by the little child
by the hand
& squeeze

You're learning
fast

Keep off the walk
listen to the children talk

Ledger domain
Wilderness pain
cruel swimming ambience
sweet swimming fish hook smile
I love you all the while
even w/the little child
by the hand
& squeeze

You're learning
fast

Keep off the walk
listen to the children talk

Cobra sun / Fever smile
—No man kill me

"Who is this insane messenger?"

In times like these we need
men around us who can
see clearly & speak the truth.

Out of breath

    Raving witness

—Who comes?
—Asia.

CASSANDRA AT THE WELL

Help! Help! Save us!
Save us!
We're dying, fella, do something.
Get us out of this!
Save us!
I'm dying.
What have we done now!
We've done it, fella, we've committed the

Help!
This is the end of us, fella.
I love you fella.
I love you fella.
I love you cause you're you.

But you've got to help us.
What have we done, fella,
What have we done now?

Where are my ~~dreamers~~ dreamers
Today & Tonight.
Where are my dancers
~~them~~ leaping madly
whirling & screaming
~~xxxxxxxx xxxxxxx~~
~~xxxxxxxx xxxxxxx~~.
Where are my women
quietly dreaming
caught like angels
on the dark porch
of ~~a xxxxxxx xxxxxx~~ ranch
~~xxx xx xxxxx~~

dance dance dance dance
dance dance dance

Where are my dreamers
Today & tonight.
Where are my dancers
leaping madly
whirling & screaming

Where are my women
quietly dreaming
caught like angels
on the dark porch
of a velvet ranch
dance dance dance dance
           dance dance dance

It was the greatest night of my life
Although I still had not found a wife
I had my friends right there beside me

Indians scattered on dawn's highway bleeding
Ghosts crowd the young child's fragile eggshell mind

We scaled the wall
We tripped thru the graveyard
Ancient shapes were all around us
No music but the wet grass
felt fresh beside the fog

Two made love in a silent spot
one chased a rabbit into the dark
A girl got drunk & made the dead
And I gave empty sermons to my head

Cemetery cool & quiet
Hate to leave
your sacred lay
Dread the milky coming of the day

In this full-throated
Sex'd cry
we must try again
to speak of the ununited
miles of sleep around
us
Bumbling thru slumber
Blind numbers

In a tiled room
We sit & brood
Refuse to move
The guards refuse

and in the last place
and in the last sweet breath
& in stroke of sine-wise crab

and in stars of plenty, stars of greed
in the written book & majesties
in fulfillment on a cliff
on the inside of butter
on smooth backs & camels
in the open vessel
in the vein
in lives untold
    who witnessed everything

For those people who died
for Nirvana
for the heavenly creed
for you, for me

These lines are written
    to convey the message
To ignore the warning
To spree upward into
Tantalizing voices
To visit under-seas
Believe
Things more horrible
                than war
Things out of the tales
Great beasts
Suffering extinction

All these monstrous
Words forsaken, falling
by all Hell
loose walls, forgotten
tumbling down into
Night/ Fast friends
fellows of the one true cross
earthly lovers crash
sweet sorrow blackness
on the spilled roadside
down, into fire
silence, cry

Argue w/breath
nice
while I cry
Midnight!

it must come
like dream
sperm
uncalled
from the center
Borderlands
where liquor's
made
flow

it must come
unbidden
like the dawn
soft haste
No hurry
hairs curl

The phone
rings
We create the dawn

I fell on the earth
        & raped the snow
I got married to life
        & breathed w/my marrow
I saw young dancers
I am meat & need fuel
Need the whorey glimmer of tears
in women, all ages
Laughter sandwich, fuel
   for the lunch of meat minds
Now damn you, dance
Now dance
or die sleek & fat in your
reeking seats, still
buckled for flight

If the writer can write, &
    the farmer can sow
Then all miracles concern,
    appear, & start happening
If the children eat, if their
    time of crying was Mid-
Night

The earth needs them
Soft dogs on the snow
Nestled in Spring
when sun makes wine
& blood dances dangerous
    in the veins of ~~the~~ vine

If the writer can write, &
 the farmer can sow
Then all miracles concur,
 appear, & start happening
If the children eat, if their
 time of crying was Mid-
 Night

The earth needs them
soft dogs on the snow
Nestled in Spring
When sun makes wine
& blood dances dangerous
 in the veins or vine

To have just come wondering
if the world is real is
sick to see the shape she's
made of.   What wandering
lunacy have we soft created?

Certain no one meant it
sure someone started
Where is he?
Where is he or it when
      we need her?
Where are you?
In a flower?

To have just been born
      for beauty & see sadness
What is this frail sickness?

———————————————

Round-up, Rondolay, Rhonda,
Red, Rich roll ruse rune
rake roan ran regard
if you know what I mean.
This is concrete imagery Vermont
The mouth leads this way
I that way
No good faster the hand too slow
To exist in time we die construct
prisms in a void
The truth   faster   These hang-ups
hold-ups   shooting the republic
The president's dream behind
The throne
four-score fast fever the clinic
the wisdom syphilis doctor nurse
Indians   americans   Atlantis
Save us   guide us   in time of need
prayer to the mind cell body
prayer to center of man   prayer
to evening's last whisper   as the
hand silently glides into peaceful
thorns   stones   storms
I await your coming
w/negligence   Speak to me!
don't leave me here alone   Torture
clinic chamber   I know the man
arrested   The stale bars   his mother
who will help a match a cigarette
I'm going. God? What is your name

There must be some way to define
stop happening space shades
postures poses snapshots   The
World behind the word & all
utterance   Can't now
coming for us   soon leave   all over
The Republic is a big cross in a
big cross the nation   The world on fire
Taxi from Africa   The Grand Hotel
He was drunk   a big party last
night there.   Pastures fields
skunks snake invisible night birds
night hawks   summer disasters
out of doors   listen to the lions
roar in the empty fields
These are forgotten
lands   Speak confidently of
the forest   the end   the joke
is on me   most certainly
There must be someone today who
knows   they do   but they can't
Tell you   like feeding a child
Wine   like sniffing cortex
blue babies lists   real estate
cleaning offices   word-vomit
mind soup   crawling lice   book bonds.

Feeling streams lead to losers
back going back in all directions
sleeping these insane hours
I'll never wake up in a good mood
again.   I'm sick of these
stinking boots.   Stories of animals
in the woods   not stupid   but
like indians peeping out   their
little eyes in the night   I know
the forest & the evil moon tide.
"We sure look funny don't we fella?"
Plu-perfect.   Forgotten.   Songs
are good streams for a laugh.
The mind bird was a good fella
Who minded labyrinths & lived
in a well   He knew Jesus
Knew Newman   Knew me &
Morganfield   I hope you can
understand these last parables
were hope (less) sure   if you can
regard them as anything beyond
matter   Surely not more than
Twice-fold fork follow & loose-
tree   Now here's the rub   rune

Rib-bait squalor the women of the
quarter yawned & meandered
swimming dust tide for food
scraps to child feed   No noon
for misses   The Church called bells
inhabitants of the well   come to hell
come to the bell   funeral jive
Negroes plenty, fluttering their
dark smiles.   Mindless lepers—
con-men   The movie is popular
This season   in all the hotels
rich tourists from the continent
shore up & hold a story seance
nightly   The birds tell & they
Know all   Telephones crooks
& castanets   The lines are wired
Listen   hear those voices & all
This long distance from the other half
I love to hear ya ramble boy
missionary stallion   One day
The devil arrived only no one tell
or you'll ruin the outcome. He
walked to the pulpit & saved
The city while certainly scoring
Someone's female daughter.
When his cloak was hoisted
The snake was seen & we all
slipped back to lethargy.

Buildings gilded no interruptions.

Constructions everywhere.   Our
own house was solid astrology
Tiny flutes won their starlings
sunrise.   And in the estuary
side-traps stopped our dinner
He came home w/bags of meat
& sacks of flour & the bread
rose & the family flourished.

Those who Race toward Death
Those who wait
Those who worry

The Endless quest a vigil
of watchtowers and fortresses
against the sea and time.
Have they won? Perhaps.
They still stand and in
their silent rooms still wander
the souls of the dead,
who keep their watch on the living.
Soon enough we shall join them.
Soon enough we shall walk
the walls of time. We shall
miss nothing
except each other.

Fence my sacred fire
I want. To be simple, black & clean
A dim nothingness
Please
The sea is green
Smoke
like the child's version of a
Christmas dream
w/no
waking.

Why the desire for death.

A clean paper or a pure
    white wall. One false
line, a scratch, a mistake.
Unerasable. So obscure
by adding million other
    tracings, blend it,
cover over.

But the original scratch
remains, written in
gold blood, shining.

Desire for a Perfect Life

As I Look Back

As I look back
over my life
I am struck by post
cards
Ruined Snap shots

faded posters
Of a time, I can't recall

I am a Scot, or so
I'm told. Really
the heir of Mystery
                    Christians

Snake in the Glen

The child of a
    Military family . . .

I rebelled against church
    after phases of
            fervor

I curried favor in school
    & attack'd the teachers

                I was given a
                desk in the corner

                I was a fool
                        &
                The smartest kid
                    in class

Walks in D.C. in
      Negro streets. The library
      & book stores. Orange
      brick in warm sun.
      The books & poets magic

Then sex gives greater stimulation
Than you've ever known &
all peace & books lose their
charm & you are thrown
back on the eye of vision

History of Rock
   coinciding w/my
            adolescence

Came to LA to
   Film School

Venice Summer

Drug Visions

Roof top songs

early struggles &
        humiliations

Thanks to the girls
who fed me.

Making Records

Elvis had sex-wise
mature voice at 19.

Mine still retains the
nasal whine of a
repressed adolescent
   minor squeaks & furies
An interesting singer
at best—a scream
or a sick croon. Nothing
in-between.

ROAD DAYS

fear of Plane death

And night was what Night
        should be
A girl, a bottle, & blessed sleep

I have ploughed
My seed thru the heart
of the nation.
    Injected a germ in the psychic blood vein.

Now I embrace the poetry
of business & become—for
a time—a "Prince of Industry"

A natural leader, a poet,
                a Shaman, w/the
soul of a clown.

What am I doing
    in the Bull Ring
            Arena
Every public figure
    running for Leader

Spectators at the Tomb
—riot watchers

Fear of Eyes
Assassination

Being drunk is a good disguise.

I drink so I
can talk to assholes.
This includes me.

The horror of business

The Problem of Money
            guilt
   do I deserve it?

The Meeting
Rid of Managers & agents

After 4 yrs. I'm left w/a
   mind like a fuzzy hammer

regret for wasted nights
   & wasted years
I pissed it all away
   American Music

End w/fond good-bye
& plans for future
—Not an actor
   Writer-filmmaker

Which of my cellves
          will be remember'd

Good-bye America
   I loved you

          Money from home
          good luck
          stay out of trouble

Afterword

James Douglas Morrison was born December 8, 1943, in Melbourne, Florida. Jim Morrison died July 3, 1971, in Paris, France.

During that span of twenty-seven years, Jim transformed himself from brilliant but recalcitrant student to poet & songwriter, from singer to rock-'n'-roll legend, from filmmaker to expatriate writer.

Jim was a working artist. He recorded seven albums of songs, most of which he wrote; he toured and performed onstage throughout the United States, Europe, Canada and Mexico; he produced two award-winning films, recorded hours of his poetry in a studio setting and published four books (including three self-published editions). Through it all he dealt with a public image that grew to outrageous and ultimately overwhelming proportions.

The constant thread in Jim's life was writing. By the summer of 1971 he had written more than sixteen hundred pages of poems, anecdotes, epigrams, lyrics, essays, stories, outlines for plays and film scripts.

For Jim, poetry was a craft to be practiced and perfected. Poems were worked and reworked, added to, subtracted from and merged with others. Drafts were edited, revised and hand-copied from one notebook to another. The process for a single poem could extend over several years and a half-dozen notebooks, yet not one page was ever dated, numbered or identified chronologically.

Our concerns while preparing Jim's poetry for publication were for accuracy and an absolute fidelity to his intentions, as far as we could discover. In order to find the last and final version of each poem, drafts were compared and studied side by side. When viewed this way, poems revealed a clear progression starting with Jim's first conceptual jottings through stages of evolution toward a complete and polished work. Many poems were never finished—works still in progress when he died.

Wilderness faithfully presents what is contained in Jim's papers and notebooks. Nothing was altered, changed, or replaced; every word and line is exactly reproduced from the original page.

Columbus B. Courson
Pearl Marie Courson

Frank Lisciandro
Katherine Lisciandro

INDEX OF FIRST LINES